HARE SOUP

D1240800

DOROTHY MOLLOY

Hare Soup

faber and faber

First published in 2004
by Faber and Faber Limited
3 Queen Square London wc1n 3au
Published in the United States by Faber and Faber Inc.
an affiliate of Farrar, Straus and Giroux LLC, New York

Typeset by Faber and Faber Limited
Printed in England by T. J. International Ltd,
Padstow, Cornwall

A CIP record for this book
is available from the British Library
ISBN 0-571-21989-6

2 4 6 8 10 9 7 5 3 1

for Andrew

Acknowledgements

Acknowledgements and thanks are due to the editors of the following journals in which some of these poems appeared for the first time: *The Dublin Review*, *Metre*, *The Cork Literary Review*, *Cyphers*, *The Shop*, *Books Ireland*, *Poetry Wales* and *Féile Filíochta* 2000.

I should also like to thank Pat Schneider, Conor O'Callaghan, John McAuliffe, Jonathan Williams, and members of the Thornfield Poets writing workshop.

Contents

HARE SOUP

Conversation Class

I redden to the roots when Jacqueline Dupont zuts
at my French. She cocks her ear and smoothes her coif and
sits me on a poof, settles herself on a chaise-longue.

'Encore une fois,' she zaps, and taps her nails and sips
her Perrier. My tongue is jammed, my teeth are in a
brace. Her hands fly to her face. 'Mon Dieu,' she cries,

'Mon Dieu, qu'est-ce qu'on peut faire?'

I fiddle with my cuticles. She checks her watch and snaps,
'Ouvrez la bouche!' Her forty clocks tick on, tick on.
Her cuckoos coil behind their yodel-flaps. Her grandfathers,

lined up against the wall, come every fifteen minutes
with a boing. 'Finie la classe!' She pours herself
a glass of Armagnac. 'Vous voulez un petit peu?'

I sluice the liquor back.

My tongue is loosed. My eyes are glazed. I sing
the *Marseillaise*. I feel a revolution
in the red flare of my skirt.

A Walk in the Forest

Electric fences hum in the forest of Fontainebleau,
disturb the twig and branch, the hand and hoof, the bristle,
and the silver-sickled tusk.

Birds avoid this place from dawn to dusk; the stags merge
with the trees. We lose our bearings in the labyrinth of leaf.
Hornets buzz around us

as we bend over the map. We cannot find the star-shaped
    clearing
where the five paths meet. I lag behind, I'm overdue.
I drag my feet. But when my waters

break, I send you forth to blaze a trail. I circle round,
ungird my loins, shake loose my hair. The sun goes down
    blood-red,
the fences spark; the bear moans

in the dark, the wild boar blinks. The night is hung with
    Zodiacs
and spiders, zinging bats. The wolves rush by in packs.
Deep in the earth I hear the vixen

cry when, doubled up, I stretch out silent arms
to catch the child that crowns between my thighs; I cut the
    cord
with teeth grown sharp as knives,

ingest the afterbirth.

Hare Soup

Monsieur Vidal is up at first light
with Kruger, his dog, shooting hares in the field
beyond where the vegetables grow.
He shatters the dawn with his gun.

Outside my window, ramshackle France.
Down in the foul-smelling kitchen, Madame.
On each page of my notebook, ahead of my scrawl,
the stink of the hare soup spreads.

At the stroke of *midi*, we sit at the table,
Monsieur and Madame Vidal, the idiot
Didier and me. I force down
the pottage. The gun-dog salivas my knee.

Didier kicks him aside, makes cow-eyes
at me. He calls me, in whispers, *coquette*,
his *jolie amie*. Sated with hare soup,
pommes frites and *compote*, black wine

and champagne, Monsieur and Madame Vidal
slump over their cups. Under the table
Kruger unsheaths his prick: a startle
of red, pencil thin, sticks out of his fur.

Didier swiftly unbuttons his flies.
He lifts up my skirt with his foot. He lunges
and tears at my blouse. I kick him aside.
When I stab at the O of his mouth with my little

canif, bouquets of old-fashioned roses
fall into my lap: petals shot with bright flashes
of scarlet and purple, vermilion, alizarin,
ruby, carmine and cerise.

Pascual the Shepherd

Down from the mountain pastures, Pascual, the shepherd,
binges at the bar.

He orders another brandy, in the singsong voice
he uses with sheep.

A young man comes in with his bride, in a flurry of snow,
to have one for the road.

Pascual raises his glass: 'Just wait till you bed her tonight
and you're snug in her fold . . .'

His tongue lollops and slurs. It cleaves to the roof of his
   mouth.
In the mirror a blur

of coiled horn rises out of his skull; and his eyes turn bright
   pink.
At the back of his head

he senses a movement of flocks; the slither of hoof
over rock, the bleat

of a lamb in the drift. Pascual shifts on the bar-stool. He
   gauges
the depth of the floor

with his fathomless feet and propels himself into the street.
Dogs howl

round his boots as he walks the tight rope of the cobbles.

Infant of Prague

I push him around in his pram. He is chalky
with lace, starched to his underskirts, taut
in his tunic and cloak.

He is ruffed at the neck, his heart hangs on his breast
like a plum; a crown holds his skull in its cincture
of gold. Flat

on his back in his princely layette, he clutches
his toy orb and cross. He fixes his gaze
on the lattice of silver

and black that comes between him and the sky.
He looks into my soul, sees the sixpence I stole
from my grandmother's purse.

He lets out a cry. I gather him up
in his ermine and scarlet. I lull him in Spanish
and Czech, brush the pale

of his cheek with my lips. Crimson embroideries
seep through his clothes; there is blood on my hands.
An ooze of vermilion

darkens the flax of his curls. Water flows
from the gash in his side. He is stiff as a statue,
his feet are stone cold.

But he glows like a little red lamp when he's back
on his plinth at the top of the stairs. He revives
like a Jericho rose.

Stigmata

On mammy's side
we were punsters and pugilists,
pillagers, prophets,
eaters of raw potatoes
and gazers at stars.

Mechtild and Hildegard, pray for me,
Francis, Theresa and John.

On daddy's side
they played roulette and Black Jack;
the one-armed bandit;
strip-poker, gin rummy,
cribbage and craps.
They went to the dogs.

Mechtild and Hildegard, pray for me,
Francis, Theresa and John.

As for me, I had visions
as soon as my breasts were in bud.
The Sacred Heart bled
on the mantel. A luminous
lady crushed snakes
with her feet. The Infant
of Prague came to call.

Mechtild and Hildegard, pray for me,
Francis, Theresa and John.

I lie on the analyst's couch,
my third eye ablaze. He tightens
his sphincter. He shrinks from my gaze.
I dig in my heels; refuse
to show him my hand: the strawberry
blood in my fist.

Mechtild and Hildegard, pray for me,
Francis, Theresa and John.

Ice Maiden

I walk in my night-dress and slippers
along winter beaches in Finland.
My earrings of polished tin
flash at the Northern Lights.
I shovel up the sea.

But the cold is quick. Quick
as I crack open the rock
of the ocean with my axe,
it freezes behind me.
My task is endless.

Family Circus

Dadda flexes his muscles. His buttons
go ping. His chest-hair springs out
of his vest. I sit mute as he lashes
at Mamma.

Mamma slumps in the chair. With her eyes
calls her infant performer, her stage-hand,
her prop. I stand firm in my sequins
and tights.

I make doe-eyes at Dadda; tap-dance,
do the splits. When the globus hystericus
swells in my throat, I swallow
my tongue.

Grandma's Zoo

There's a zoo in Grandma's pocket:
horse and bull, fish and bird,
stag, pig and rabbit. Hound.

When I stay with Grandma,
she takes an animal out of her pocket
and gives it to me:

a charm against the foghorns
booming on the pier;

a charm against the steam-engines
whistling in the dark;

a charm against the elephant-man
who comes bellowing to my bed.

'Was it like this?'

Beatrix cried
when a strange man forced his way
into her room, put his hand
up her jersey, his tongue
in her mouth, tore
at her skirt and gave her
a jolt. Blood on her shoe.

Beatrix cried
when she told her boyfriend
all about
what the strange man did.

'Was it like this?' her boyfriend asked.
His voice was strange. He pushed her hard
against the wall, put his hand
up her jersey, his tongue
in her mouth, tore
at her skirt and gave her
a jolt. Blood on her other shoe.

Beatrix cried.

Eternity Ring

I can't get this blasted thing off:
the ring set with stones that eats into

my flesh. I've tried fretsaws and slashers
and pneumatic drills; Fatima,

butter and soap. Lard.
I rode a tank over my knuckles,

I dropped a bomb onto my hand.
The ring is still grand.

'Long time no see'

I met Laura in the field,
looking pale behind her glasses.
Was she weeping in the grasses?
I met Laura in the field.

I was strolling in my wellingtons,
my anorak and woolly cap.
I didn't want her kind of crap.
I was strolling in my wellingtons.

She said, 'Long time no see.
He's gone again, that bastard Matt.'
I replied: 'Well, fancy that.'
She said, 'Long time no see.'

I could have said: 'He's in my bed.'
I could have told her, but I didn't.
I nearly told her, but I didn't.
I could have said: 'He's in my bed.'

I met Laura in the field,
looking pale behind her glasses.
Was she weeping in the grasses?
I met Laura in the field.

Small Wedding

They wanted a small wedding. Found a priest
who did it for a song. They gave each other
barmbrack rings; a pea, a bean, a stick, a rag;
a Christmas cracker joke, a paper-hat.

He wore a pin-striped suit with wide lapels
and ankle flares. She wore her polka-dots.

Her bouquet was a dandelion; his buttonhole
a daisy; the wedding breakfast, ice-cream
on a doily with a peach.

Jenny moved a mountain just to be there.
Stephen made a speech.

Floating with Mr Swan

Mr Swan, the anaesthetist, jabs at my arm
till I'm jelly-leg, head-flop and flap-wing.

He bears me aloft in his beak. He plucks
at my pubes. Kisses me on a mouth

that won't pucker or purse. My tongue is a wodge
of wet paper. My plasticene lips

don't belong on my face. My words are a slur of
'I wuv ya. I wuv ya.' He fiddles

with tubes, takes out his syringe. Then he rises
to meet me. Like Leda, I wait for

his thrust. All I get is a slap on the cheek
from the nurse with the upside-down watch

and the back-to-front hands.

First Blood

Après-dîner we sip anisette.
You tell me your stories of paradise
lost. I tell you of tennis-club
hops, Auld Lang Syne and a mistletoe
kiss.

Your lids at half-mast, you refill
my glass. I put on my rose-coloured
specs. I tell you of Antoine,
the bold boy from France, my heart
like a fizz-bag

when he squeezed my hand. How we danced
that last dance! Comatose in the dead
heat, you stare at your plate:
'Et alors?' I tell you of nibblings
in kitchens

at midnight, of shocking-pink lipstick
that glowed in the dark, the ultra-fine
mesh of my first fish-net stockings,
the mess of my feet in my first high-heeled
shoes.

I tell you of camisoles slotted
with ribbons, my first full-length dress
made of satin and lace; the mugs
of hot coffee, the Aga, the clothes-horse,
the starch

in my petticoat, the rouge on my face
when I felt the first frisson of fur.
You beat a tattoo on the table,
you 'psst' at the waiter to flag down
a cab,

push me back on the leatherette seat.
I am weak at the knees. Fast forward
and freeze.

Cut.

At the back of my head a camera
pans over the scene. Someone
is opening the door of my house
with a scalding hot key. There is blood
on the floor.

Someone is screaming 'For each one
you fucked'. Someone is calling me
'Whore'.

Black Flies

Sister Cherubina, lumpy
in her habit, rosary beads
snarling at her ankles,
scoops cold tea-leaves
out of a bucket.

Black flies on the floor.

Trapped on a high stool,
behind locked doors, I racket
at a grand piano; fingers slippery
on keys of blackberry
and meringue.

Black flies on the staves.

Sister Cherubina humps past
the music room.
I hear the bucket clang.

Mother Anastasia beats time
with her stick: raps me
on the knuckles.

Black flies fill my eyes.

I can't find my feet.

The Woman and the Hill

Clad only in oilskins, I ride a man's bike,
glide along with reptilian sloth.

Chin on the handlebars, a swaddle of hair
on my back, my comatose lids

are like lead. When I get to the hill, I dismount,
hide my bike in the gorse. I pedal

the buttery slope with my antediluvian
feet. For aeons I treadmill

in place till a ladder of roots pulls me into
the trees. I grow dark as the forest

slides over my face. I visit the sett
of the badger, the lair of the fox;

adore the wild sow on her altar of wood.
I slough off my skin. The wind gathers

my hair in its snood. From peep-holes high up
in the bone of my head, the eyes of a goshawk protrude.

Family Get-together

Only one little bitch can cross the divide
between us. Hands reach out

from separate worlds to touch her fur.
She can curl up on anybody's

lap. She gets the soft side
of everybody's tongue.

But lookie here. See these,
our hearts, come straight from the butcher's

hook. They hang on our chests
like rubies, wrapped in cellophane

and twine, with big red blobs
of sealing-wax to guarantee them

tamper-proof.

In the makeshift village cinema

The stalls are kitchen chairs. They're no good
for courting. The adults above on the balcony
watch every move.

We crack sunflower seeds between our teeth,
feel each other sideways through pockets
full of hands,

all thumb; shed our shoes, play footsie
under the seat. We talk back to the stars
on the screen,

smack our lips at the celluloid kisses,
crunch out at the interval on carpets
of husk,

escape to the street. The crash
of the river masks our sweet nothings
as we squeeze

in the dark. Jolted by the bell
for Part Two, we grope our way back
with red cheeks.

The voyeurs in the gods settle down
and the show must go on. As the amateur
usherette

fades with her torch, we resolve
to strip off this tight valley tonight
and make it

over the highest peak

                    into France.

French Hotel

We get there through the blinding fields of rape.
Dinner is late.
Pâté de foie gras, a piece of veal:
cold cuts
upon a plate. Dusty wine. Crusty bread.

Madame is pregnant; Monsieur is *en garde*
behind the till.
A serving-girl, too shy to speak, can only take
our order
for dessert. A trifling thing. *Compote.*

The rain drops on the corrugated roof.
The dark magnolia
opens up her cup beside the trough.
Insomniac,
the orphaned calves, the bonny-clabbered cows

with bursting teats, the honking force-fed geese
swirl
in my head. To while away the wee small hours,
I swat mosquitoes;
count the corpses on the blood-stained ceiling of this small hotel.

It's croissants, *comme toujours*, for breakfast; pots
of *confiture*,
café au lait. We check the etymology
of Fontainebleau.
'Belle eau', says the *patron*. 'C'est ça. Bien sûr.'

We bid a fond *adieu*. Unfold our map. Swear
we'll be back.
Drive south, as planned, to do the Côte d'Azur.

Near Sagunto

Splitting the curtain of beads, she welcomes me in,
her rope soles soft on the flags.

She speaks in a strange tongue, English a strain
on her lips after so many years.

Husband and sons dark as figs, her mulberry daughters
are silky as cats at her feet.

She has ripened in the heat. Except for the pile of bright
    hair
on her head and the blue eyes that hide

in the flap of her fan, she is Mediterranean now,
at home in their olive ways.

It might have been me had I stayed, strolling in spring-time
through acres of pink almond trees,

seeking in summer the shade of my own orange grove.
But

the north wind havocs my face. I no longer belong
in this place.

Tramontana

In Cadaqués the women with red arms and pickled hands
    salt anchovies.
The fishermen, marooned in bars, smoke fat cigars; play
    chess and dominoes.
The tramontana rattles doors and shutters. Waves crash on
    harbour walls.
The people here go mad. They blame the wind.

You throw logs on the fire; pine-cones for resin, sizzle,
    incense-rise.
You scrape the hard-wood palette with a knife, burn off
    old paint, toil
with your rags and turps. Half-faint, turn to the sink, pour
    in the bleach.
The people here go mad. They blame the wind.

The tramontana strips the beach of sand. The storks are
    gone. Gone the swallows
from their mid-flight resting-place beneath your arch. Gone
    south to Zanzibar.
I climb the steep steps to the terraced roof. A frieze of pines
    screens out
the white-horsed sea. Rough passage waits for me, as I go
    north.
The people here go mad. They blame the wind.

Stalemate

Because I swam nude in the sea on midsummer's night,
you sulked for a year on your bed in the Street of the Fig.

Now on the Eve of St John two thousand and one,
you and I, Baldomero, are still at our posts, daggers drawn.

Fool's Gold

You drew me naked as I sat,
my shoulders straight, my head held high,
my face turned to the light.

You took me in with narrowed eyes
when I lay down, half-hid in shade.
Your pencil caught me on the page.

You drew us fusing at the lips,
afloat above the chimney-pots,
my head flung back, my night-dress loose,

my bracelets glinting in the clair
de lune.

In Montserrat you pledged your troth
upon Assumption Day.
The flags, the stones, the dumb bells

of the ancient church bore witness,
and the silent stained-glass windows
wrote it down. And it was done.

Done.

I kept your promise in a pyx,
a bubble on a swizzle stick,
long after you had gone.

I keep it in a shoebox now,
fool's gold, protected from the light,
along with First Communion snaps

and rosaries with pearly beads,
and baby teeth the fairy-folk
forgot.

Sea-bitch

She softens in the sea. Loses the shape
of her clothes.

Always the black elephant swimming beside her.
The short-snouted porpoise

buttering her up. Blubbery as a seal
in salt water,

she lets me touch the purple jellyfish of her heart;
leaves her sting

in the melt of my hand. Sea-bitch, I have come half-way
to meet you.

Looking for Mother

I ransack her room. Loot and pillage.
I root in her trunk. Crack open
the tightly sprung boxes of satin
and plush. Pierce my breast with her butterfly

brooch. I pose in her hats,
French berets, mantillas of lace,
the veil that falls over her face,
the boa she wraps round her neck.

I try on her shoes. Her slippers
are mules. I can't walk in her callipered
boots. I break into her wardrobe.
Hands grope in the dark. Faded bats,

like umbrellas, are humming inside.
Stoles of fox-fur and mink: tiny claws,
precise nails. Lips clamped in the rictus
of death. I'm hot on the scent

of oestrus, umbilicus, afterbirth,
eau-de-cologne. I fling myself
down on the bed that she made
of dirt from the Catacombs, blood

of the saints. Under the counterpane,
nettles, goose-feathers, a torc.

Plaint

I've prayed with others of my ilk at Canterbury,
Compostela, Montserrat. In Walsingham
I've kissed the vial of Virgin's milk, the silky bones
of Madeleine in Vézelay, the Baby Jesus'
swaddling clothes in La Chapelle. And now in Chartres
I fast, and try my luck.

I kneel before the altar where *La Sainte Chemise*
is glowing in its box. Light a candle to the
Lady on the Pillar juggling with the flaming
hearts. The Count of Dreux salutes me as I
pass. The King of France looks up from braiding
Blanche's hair, and nods.

I don the pilgrim's conch. I beat my breast;
betake myself to Martyrs' Well, sink through the liquid
core of Holy Mountain, full eighteen fathoms
deep. Angels weigh my soul on scales
of air and lead and glass. I read the stars
and weep. I cross myself

au nom du Père, du Fils, du Saint Esprit.
The gargoyles leer. A donkey plays the hurdy-gurdy
on a plinth. Women heel and toe it round
the labyrinth. I follow in bare feet.
My blind soles catch the rhythm as they touch the black
on white. I go to Golgotha

and back. I count the ninety doors in this
Cathedral. I trace the masons' signatures
on stone. I find the steps, a thousand treads,
that spiral to the roof. Rose-windows spin
above the graven apse where Mary
births her baby in the cave

at Bethlehem. The Wise Men gather round with
precious gifts. The angels pause mid-flight.
Prostrate before the Child, I make my plaint.
The Virgin intercedes. She lets me stroke
Le Saint Prépuce. The marble bleeds.
I sing the great Amen.

Cast Out

She wears a black cowl round her head, her grey hem sweeps
    the dust.
She circles my walled city with her clappers and her cup.

From battlement and organ-loft I throw her food to eat:
unleavened bread, goat's cheese, the flesh of swine. But God
    forbid

she draw the water from my well or raise her lips to mine.
I fill my mouth with cloves. I hold my nose. I breathe into

a handkerchief of lace. All night I hear her pace.
I douse myself with vinegar, rose-water, eau-de-vie.

She calls my name. She rattles at the locks. She drinks the slurry
from the trough. She shadows me in dreams. I pray to God,

'Oh let it end. Enough!' She's shed her eyebrows, lost her sense
of touch. Her voice is like the toad's. The priests call out

'Leviticus, Leviticus'; perform her funeral rite,
as it behoves, beside the fresh-dug pit. The coffin waits;

the winding-sheet, the spices and the spade; the carrion crow.
I sprinkle her with clay, ignore her cries. I turn away

to ring the Requiem bell. She joins the living dead.
At Mass I see her lean into the leper-squint, receive

from some gloved hand the Sacred Host. Until Christ comes
    to rest
upon my tongue, I live in dread. My palace is a Spittle House.

I wear beneath my robe her running sores. Under my hood,
her face.

Lady of Sorrows

Knives in her chest,
the Lady of Sorrows
glows in her niche.

He has marched off again,
the little tin soldier,
banging his drum. Ratatat.

No kiss could detain him,
no love-bite on earlobe
or nape. There is work

to be done. Ratatat.
He blows hot down the telephone,
sends her a dildo from France.

She pukes on his pillow,
pulls knives from her chest,
throws the gold ring away.

He comes goose-stepping back,
a gun in his pocket.
Work to be done. Ratatat.

In the outhouse he plugs her
– love-bites on earlobe
and nape – shoots himself

in the crotch.
The Lady of Sorrows
glows in her niche.

King's Paramour

I scour the meadows for rue; dam the place
where he'll come with a compress of willow and juniper,
feverfew, white hellebore.

When he withdraws, I leap out of bed,
drink a flagon of sweet basil tea; burn over
hot coals the hoof of a mule;

swallow dittany, caper-spurge, marjoram, iris;
sit still, watch the moon. If needs be, I provoke
the red gush with mandrake and scammony,

colocynth, lavender, gentian and thyme.
If I grow big, I draw out the fruit
of my womb (as I must) with a poultice

of acorns and irises, burdock and dill.
Still, whether the Queen remain barren
or no, next year I'll bear him

a son; catch a hare, kill a pig. But tonight
(cross my heart, swear to die) I will smear my dark lips
with sisymbrium, cyclamen, unicorn dung.

Let him come.

Les Grands Seigneurs

Men were my buttresses, my castellated towers,
the bowers where I took my rest. The best and worst
of times were men: the peacocks and the cockatoos,
the nightingales, the strutting pink flamingos.

Men were my dolphins, my performing seals; my sailing-ships,
the ballast in my hold. They were the rocking-horses
prancing down the promenade, the bandstand
where the music played. My hurdy-gurdy monkey-men.

I was their queen. I sat enthroned before them,
out of reach. We played at courtly love:
the troubadour, the damsel and the peach.

But after I was wedded, bedded, I became
(yes, overnight) a toy, a plaything, little woman,
wife, a bit of fluff. My husband clicked
his fingers, called my bluff.

Props for the Parting Scene

I catch the last train. Hang from the strap.

You stay hunched on the receding platform
like a spy: a beard glued to your chin,

eyes behind shades, a newspaper you feign interest in,
as I hurtle down the track;

watch you grow small.

ubray Bookshop
un Laoghaire
hopping centre
el: 01 280 9917
AT: IE 8217 5610

-01-02 15:27   SALE   2 0435
ERATOR

RODUCT	QTY	HSE VAT
ate 5000	1	13.50 2

| 2491 8611 | 13.50 | 13.50 |

	1	
Total	1	13.50
CASH		50.00
TOTAL TENDERED		50.00
CHANGE		36.50

ease keep receipt for exchange
credit note

Ventriloquist's Dummy

You lever my jaws, make your claptrap
shoot from my mouth. There's a stamping
of feet. Wolf-whistles. Catcalls.

I burn, turn my face from the crowd
when I feel your thumb press on my gusset,
your falsetto rise in my throat.

Offstage, I gag when you come
on the stump of my tongue. You project
not a sound through my lips till I action

my jaws, spit your codpiece back into
your lap. Then the roaring begins.
Between us we bring the house down.

Still Life with Balcony

In this photograph you are three.
You sit on a chair, frowning,
hiding your broken teeth.

You are wearing a hand-knit jersey
with your initials on the chest.
They say you did not cry

when you discovered papa dead.
You clung to mamma's skirts.
But up she leaped,

made for the balcony,
dragging you behind her,
fingers tangled in her pleats.

She billowed like a sail
as she plunged; your hand
clutched at thin air as you

smashed into the wrought-iron
rail. Uncle Pedro reeled you in
like a fish;

blood in your mouth.

Mad about José

Anna went mad when she met José.
She threw off her diamonds, glass slippers, mink coat.
She put on an apron. She scrubbed his floor.
Her knees swelled up like purple hearts.

One midnight he fell in the door, fumbling
with cufflinks and flies. Anna loosened his tie
and put him to bed. Undaunted by bristle
and reek, the rasp of his tongue, she asked

for a kiss. His fist on her backbone, he pushed himself
in. Knuckled down, cracked her sternum, came yelping,
his paws on her rump. Then collapsed in a coma,
his face to the wall. Anna licked herself down,

washed him off. On the cusp of each breast, bruises
like rainbows, blue, purple and black. She bent over
the sink. She pounded his handkerchief. Mangled
his Y-fronts. Gyrating around with the handle,

she just could not stop, till she thought of the knot
she would make in his tie as he slept. Funny
how quick he turned blue, purple, black. Anna dressed
in her diamonds, glass slippers, mink coat. Left her knees

and her apron. No note.

It happened in Parque Güell

In Parque Güell water gushes
from the mouths of salamanders;
minarets sparkle in the sun.

You took me thirty-six times
in my dress of lavender and pink,
my hem frothy at the knee.

He took me once; his head
in a black tent, his tripod
sizzling in the heat.

He threw my image in a bucket,
offered me a baby
while we waited.

The lace at the end of my dress
weighed me down. I merged
with the mosaics.

He gave me my picture
in a cardboard frame.
'You like?'

My hand shook
as I offered him silver
in exchange.

Postulant

The cloister hems the novice in;

the fountain laughs, the well is deep.
She cannot sleep. She wraps the wimple
round her head, her cheeks,
her chin and neck. Behind the iron
grille she hears his step.

For morning Mass he chooses her
to vest him in the chasuble
and alb. He calls her
'Friend in Christ' and puts the host
upon her tongue. She grips her beads

and guards her eyes. He beckons her
again to hold The Book,
to ring the bell, to pour the water,
fill the cup; to feed the incense-burner
with the olibanum, styrax

and the cascarilla bark.

I saved them in mid-winter

I saved them in mid-winter.
Sat a boiling kettle on the ice
to melt a ring of air
so they could breathe.

Mint, weed and stone. Black water.

It could have been a cat.
Some say a heron got them
or that they died of fright
when crazed, in her first heat,
my bitch jumped in the pond.

Mint, weed and stone. Black water.

The fish just disappeared.
The staring palm-tree knows;
the honeysuckle, ivy plant,
geranium, hydrangea.

Mint, weed and stone. Black water.

I was quite fond of one:
a hunch-backed carp. He used to raise
his head above the murk
to get a pet; his rounded fish-mouth
open for a kiss.

Mint, weed and stone. Black water.

Burial

I made a little coffin
for my womb,
of hardwood, lined with velveteen
and plush.

I went to my own funeral,
behind the garden
shed; summoned angels
to escort me

into Paradise. The honeysuckle
wept.
The purple fuchsia bled
upon the ground.

I rang the blue-bells loud.
And in the hush
I cut the sod and sank the box
and topped it

with a stone. Lilies sprouted
in the grass:
Amaranthus, Agapanthus,
Amaryllis.

Snapdragons guard the spot.

The Photograph

The photograph
on your memorial card
is darker than the original,

smudged – a carbon copy.

Someone's black thumbprints
have been all over your face:
you're hard to see, getting

fainter all the time.

Passage

The teased-up earth
settles.
Nettles sting
in the ducts.

We buried you
today.
Firmed you
in.

The grass seed is
down.
The water
poured.

There is a stir
among the stars:

a cosmic shift;
a making way.

Earthing

The vet gave her back to me
in a jar eight inches tall,
so heavy, my heart sank
under the weight.

When I poured her into the earth,
a blur of fur and bone
slipped through my fingers
like silk.

By August, the lid of her grave
was lush again,
marked only by distance
from flagstone and shrub.

I measure her whereabouts now
in the span of my hands
over grass, track her in the sands
of time.

Playing the Bones

The bones I feel inside my skin
are scaffolding that holds me in.

Earth will glean them when I'm chaff,
and wafted off.

Those bones will be an implement,
an ornament or instrument.

Fingers will wrap themselves around
the hollow sound.

They'll play the bones *fortissimo*,
disturb me when I'm lying low.

Intent on resurrection – spring,
or some such thing.

Envelope of Skin

In an envelope of skin,
in a box of bone
I live. Jointed arms,
legs, fingers, toes,
ankles, elbows,
shoulders. The small
shovels of my collarbone.
The caterpillar of my
spine. The wide plates
of my hips.

In an envelope of skin,
in a box of bone
I live. Endless skeins
of hair push through
the epidermis. A hundred
years' supply of nail crouches
inside my fingertips
and under the cushions
of my toes.

Drums hide in the swirl
of my ear; a bridge
crosses my nose.

My belly a factory,
a recycling plant,
a compost heap.
My pelvis a girdle,
a breeding-ground,
a nursery.

The sponges of my lungs,
the pump of the heart,
the pulse at wrist
and neck
and temple.

Alone in my cave
I quest, striking matches
as I go. Paintings
in blood and excrement glow
on my palaeolithic walls.

Itineraries of Gold

Elephants, embroidered in silk,
circle the hem of my skirt.
On my upper arm, the bangles.
In the centre of my forehead,
the painted sign.
Around my neck, the gold.

Frowning, you walk beside me,
counting your profits
on an abacus of precious stones.
Until the sickle moon cuts
through the night sky,
you will not rest.

Then your brown fingers
will uncover the abacus
of my body: its taut wires,
its precious stones.

Outside our tent, elephants
will sink to their knees,
lean into the sand;
heavy in their garments
of ivory and leather.

Sweet Nothings

Your kisses were marshmallow
osculations on my lips,
in the lapse between the
conversation lozenges.

His were gelatinous confections,
rum and butter,
caramels.

Dark liqueurs, bilabial plosives,
glottal stops.
Honey-drops to suck

till cock-crow, when he gave me
fricatives.
Set

love-bites round my neck
like fudge; filled me
with Turkish Delight (Oh Haji Bey!).

Left me
a jelly baby.

Postman's Knock

Your letters are like folded moons on onionskin,
suns pleated into envelopes, opaque Mallorcan
pearls.

You send me things: a diamond ring, a glass
of pink champagne, an antique fan, a high comb
for my hair.

You send me water from the Canaletas fountain;
ripe apricots at Christmas, marzipan
for January the Sixth.

The seasons come and go. You send me virgin snow
from Nuria, a piece of ancient rock
from Montserrat;

the songs of Lluis Llach. I lie in bed
all day at fever pitch and wait
for postman's knock.

The propositions that he pushes through the letterbox
(along with your dispatches) land
like homing-pigeons

in the hall; drive me insane
with their damn *cu-cu-ru-cu-cú*.

Chacun à son goût

I went to Chartres for windows; angled my neck
to the stained light.

You did your cathedral thing: merged
with the oak pew;

lowered your lids over eyes blue as the glass.